CAT COUPLES

CAT COUPLES

JOAN BARON

Harper & Row, Publishers, New York
Cambridge, Philadelphia, San Francisco, London
Mexico City, São Paulo, Sydney

On the front cover: POPCORN AND HAMBURGER
On the back cover: EDNA AND HENRY
Frontispiece: BARNABY AND GOAT CAT

CAT COUPLES. Copyright © 1983 by Joan Baron. All rights reserved. Printed in the United States of America. No part of this book may be used or reproduced in any manner whatsoever without written permission except in the case of brief quotations embodied in critical articles and reviews. For information address Harper & Row, Publishers, Inc., 10 East 53rd Street, New York, N.Y. 10022. Published simultaneously in Canada by Fitzhenry & Whiteside Limited, Toronto.

FIRST EDITION

Designer: Gloria Adelson/LuLu Graphics

Library of Congress Cataloging in Publication Data

Baron, Joan.
  Cat couples.

  (Harper colophon books)
  1. Cats—Pictorial works. I. Title.
SF446.B37 1983   779'.32   82-48798
ISBN 0-06-090986-2 (pbk.)

83 84 85 86 87 10 9 8 7 6 5 4 3 2 1

For Howie

ACKNOWLEDGMENTS

I am particularly grateful to my editor Larry Ashmead, who gave me the opportunity to photograph and fantasize about my favorite creatures.

I am indebted also to Pat O'Brien and Ed Lee of Photographics Unlimited; to Marc Ajello, Terry Baron, Kay Johnson, Abby Morrison and Sally White for invaluable assistance in certain locations; and to Arlene, Elizabeth and Stephen Fischer, Elizabeth Hamilton, Joan Konner, Scott Manning, Leonore Fleischer, Anita Ellis, Craig Nelson, and Bernard A. Weisberger for suggestions which have been incorporated here. And thanks to Ani Chamichian who suggested the theme of this book.

My thanks to all the cat lovers, and to the few agnostics too, who provided me with leads. And special thanks to those cat people who generously allowed me to spend time in their homes taking pictures of their beloved pets. I realize many would have been less anxious and/or self-conscious sitting for portraits themselves.

Since it is the nature of cats to do exactly as they please, this book would not have been possible without their cooperation. To each of the hundreds of cats I met in connection with *Cat Couples,* I send a little rub behind the ears to express my appreciation.

AN OBSERVATION

Cat couples form relationships
That warrant our reflection—

When strange cats meet
They hesitate
As each one holds inspection.

Sometimes they spar, strength dominates,
The conquered flees or cowers.
From that time on, to have his way
The victor merely glowers.

But when there's no rejection
In this ritual inspection,
Their icy bearings slowly melt
And give way to affection.

Then clowns, they play
At scare and snare,
And cuddle up for hours.

And never will a feline pair
Know early love that sours.

MAGGIE AND **NICKY**

"There goes the neighborhood."

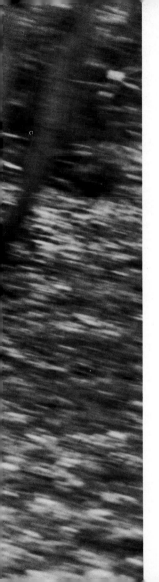

HECKEL AND JECKEL

"Wabbit!"

JULIE AND SNOWFLAKE

"Let's split—this place freaks me out in daylight."

CHAMPION AND SAMSON

"Here comes Henri Rousseau with his easel again."

JUDY AND CHEESY

"Dining al fresco has a certain . . . je ne sais quoi."

CALEDONIA AND TOM-TOM

"En garde!"

SOX AND **FLUFFERNUT**

"Because it's there."

ARLO AND ERNIE

"Surf's Up!"

WAIF AND STRAY

". . . and STAY out!"

TUXEDO AND RAPUNZEL

"Just keep puffing and glaring—his bark is worse than his bite."

CATO AND **RADAR**

"Stay cool; I got us out, I'll get us in."

PRIDE AND JOY

"OK, you get under the covers, I'll walk on her face."

ARNOLD AND **SYLVIA**

"Take the silver! Take the jewelry! Then for God's sake, get out and leave us alone!"

ARLO AND ERNIE

"Get set, you take the one on the left . . ."

Blast off!

MUFFY AND CHIP

"Get ahold of yourself—it's a lousy little cockroach!"

ORIS AND REFLECTION

"So you look a little tired and you're not a kitten anymore."

ANATOLE AND PUMPKIN

"If they find us, let me handle it."

NATASHIA AND SPIKE

"They're taking this chair to be upholstered! Part of my *life* is going with it!"

MOUSE AND C2

"Pot-au-feu? I don't know exactly, but I think it means we're getting bumped."

CAPTAIN AND SHOES

"It'll be at least another half-hour—our bowls are in the dishwasher."

99 AND SATCH

"Two hundred calories a day! That vet wants to kill us."

MS. MISSY AND MR. ULYSSES

"I can think of no greater pleasure in life than curling up on a good book."

MONARCH AND CHANCE

"Must you *always* tear through the papers?"

POO-POO AND BONES

ABBY AND **GEORGIE**

"Buzz off!"

JEEP AND TIGER

"I said it's my turf."

COLLETE AND **O.J.**

"Sometimes things just don't work out."

JEFFERSON AND RUFUS

"I'm just a very decorative companion. He'll never get over his first mate."

BARNABY AND TULIP

"Do you think twin beds is the answer?"

BOOTSIE AND FLUFFY

"It was rotten from the beginning."

SANCHO PANZA AND DULCINEA

"Nibble my ear and I'll follow you anywhere."

HUDSON AND PAL

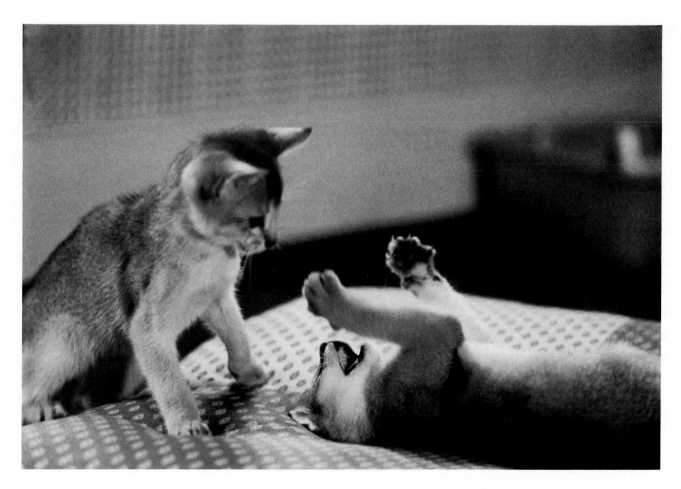

"C'mon, we'll take turns. No shiatsu, just a rubdown. Then I'll do you!"

BRANDY AND ABIGAIL

"Hey, they're playing our song."

TARRAH AND PETE

"Sorry."

DANDY AND SANDY

"What a hard day's night!"

SANCHO PANZA AND **DULCINEA**

EDNA AND **HENRY**

BELLE WATLING AND JONAS WILKERSON

"Shall I dim the lights . . . a little soft music?"

WOODY AND **SPOT**

"Ah, sweet mystery of life, at last I've found you . . ."

NIKKO AND DAIQUIRI

"I thought he was away this week!"

RERE AND LILI

"She knows I'm craaazy about her!"

CALLI AND TUCKER

"What do you expect? I've been through the wringer!"

RAMSES II AND DANIEL

"C'mon Pops—you carouse around all night, of course you feel rough in the morning."

PETE AND CATTY

"The vet says you are very lucky, thanks God. And now maybe you got that hot tin roof nonsense out of your system."

SMOKEY AND **SUNNY**

"The holidays always get me down."

OMAR AND NEWTON

"But I *need* you. You have everything to live for."

RASTUS AND ROCK

"We'll be together *forever.*"

ERNIE AND BRIT

"Whoops!"

OBJET AND ERNIE

A PHILOSOPHY

Folks who think art copies nature
Are mistaken from the start.
See how cats behave like statues?
Clearly, nature copies art.

SLY OF FOXTAIL AND BOO

PETE AND *OBJET*

"Man, talk about *frigid.*"

TAIPAN AND LAMA

"How *dare* you say such a thing!"

ARLO AND ERNIE

SMOKEY AND SUNNY

"Take that . . ."

RHETT AND **SAMMIE**

". . . and that!"

LITTLE JOEY AND BIG JOEY

". . . and that!"

SLY OF FOXTAIL AND BOO

"Oh, it hurts so good!"

THE KITTEN AND THE PUSSY-CAT

The Kitten and the Pussy-Cat went to sea
On a beautiful pea-green float:
They felt uneasy and a little bit queasy
And shelter seemed ever remote.
Then Pussy looked up at the trees beyond
And thought, "They don't look that far.
I can run for the woods where it's shady, my love
What beautiful shade trees they are
They are
They are!
What beautiful shade trees they are!"

Pussy said to the Kitten, "Let's run like the dickens,
You'd better come too, or you'll sink!"
And she dashed for the wood as fast as she could
And landed, all fours, in the drink!

On the float Kitten stayed, on the float Kitten prayed,
And Pussy will never forget
That swimming's no fun when you're trying to run.

There was never a Pussy so wet
So wet
So wet!
There was never a Pussy so wet!

PUTSCHKE AND PETE

ON GENETICS

With Eastern secrets well concealed
Top cats from Siam crossed the seas
To meet their silky cousins—
The sable brown Burmese.

PSYCHE AND ATHENA

PIXIE AND **RHETT**

Well, they mixed up their genes,
Their coats they blended,
Grey cats, blacks and whites descended.
(Stripes and spots were most engendered.)

Sooner or later all breeds get together—
Some freely, some chosen for class.
Cats are somewhat less fancy
When mating is chancy
And kittens spring up from the grass.

ARLO AND ERNIE

But calicos, tabbies, exotics and alleys
Are kindred despite their begats.
All harbor through history
The Orient's mystery.

Inscrutable

Secretive

Cats.

MAI AND **TOM**

KATE AND FIDEL

"All right, you're beautiful, but can you act?"

CHARLES DARWIN AND GREGOR MENDEL

". . . and then peel me a grape."

TURBO AND PITTYWITS

"Tonight I'll cover the pâté, you work the shrimp."

SIRIO AND SCHLOMO

"I wouldn't mind the wait so much if The Green Thumb sold one single thing *we* could eat."

SAMMY SABLE AND SHEBA

"I know the others get to play in the street, darling, but you know we're not *like* the others."

MISSY AND **SAM**

"Sure you've been to London to visit the Queen—and I'm Dick Whittington's cat!"

HEATHCLIFFE AND OLMO

FRODO AND MSFIT

DANDY AND SANDY

BARNABY AND GOAT CAT

DYAN AND **TIGER**

"Where have all the flowers gone?"

CAST OF CHARACTERS

ABBY AND GEORGIE	Clara Graedel, *New York, New York*
ANATOLE AND PUMPKIN	Sann and John Van Deventer, Jr., *Southampton, New York*
ARLO AND ERNIE	Terry and Michael Baron, *New Orleans, Louisiana*
ARNOLD AND SYLVIA	Stuart Harris, *New York, New York*
BARNABY AND GOAT CAT	Matilda M. Dobbs, *Atlanta, Georgia*
BARNABY AND TULIP	Ms. Phyllis S. Levy, *New York, New York*
BELLE WATLING AND JONAS WILKERSON	Betty Talmadge, *Lovejoy, Georgia*
BOOTSIE AND FLUFFY	Robyn Binstein and Liz Goldsmith, *Englewood, New Jersey*
BRANDY AND ABIGAIL	JoAnne and Bobby Putnam, *Atlanta, Georgia*
CALEDONIA AND TOM-TOM	Helen Mewborn, *Tucker, Georgia*
CALLI AND TUCKER	J. Louis Harris, D.V.M., *Tucker, Georgia*
CAPTAIN AND SHOES	Mrs. William Paul Mallard (Cindy), *Atlanta, Georgia*
CATO AND RADAR	Cathie and Dean Schaffer, *Mt. Kisco, New York*
CHAMPION AND SAMSON	The Housepians, *Englewood, New Jersey*
CHARLES DARWIN AND GREGOR MENDEL	Sylvia Brody-Axelrod, *New York, New York*

COLLETE AND **O.J.**	George Caldwell and George Castello, *East Hampton, New York*
DANDY AND **SANDY**	Mara, Careth, Ayren and A.J. Moskowitz, *Great Barrington, Massachusetts*
DYAN AND **TIGER**	Joel Weinstein, *East Hampton, New York*
EDNA AND **HENRY**	Jane Howard, *Sag Harbor, New York*
ERNIE AND **BRIT**	Terry and Michael Baron, *New Orleans, Louisiana*
FRODO AND **MSFIT**	Mrs. Sewell K. Loggins (Mary), *Atlanta, Georgia*
HEATHCLIFFE AND **OLMO**	Suzanne Levine and Robert Levine, *New York, New York*
HECKEL AND **JECKEL**	Shirley Baty, *Water Mill, New York*
HUDSON AND **PAL**	Lawrence P. Ashmead/Phyllis Goldman, *New York, New York*
JASMINE'S KITTENS	James D. Baron, *Bridgehampton, New York*
JEEP AND **TIGER**	Sally and Sam Brody, *Brooklyn Heights, New York*
JEFFERSON AND **RUFUS**	Wilfrid Sheed and Miriam Ungerer, *Sag Harbor, New York*
JUDY AND **CHEESY**	Margaret Phillips, *Atlanta, Georgia*
JULIE AND **SNOWFLAKE**	June Peretti, *Englewood, New Jersey*
KATE AND **FIDEL**	Jill and Roger Caras/Phyllis Barclay, *East Hampton, New York*
LITTLE JOEY AND **BIG JOEY**	Melissa and Billy Halsey, *Water Mill, New York*
MAGGIE AND **NICKY**	Carolyn Bryson, *Decatur, Georgia*
MAI AND **TOM**	Marilyn P. Dornbush, *Atlanta, Georgia*
MISSY AND **SAM**	Nancy I. Williams, *Sag Harbor, New York*

MONARCH AND CHANCE	Brenda Lloyd, *Decatur, Georgia*
MOUSE AND C2	Paul and Ann Hill, *Atlanta, Georgia*
MS. MISSY AND MR. ULYSSES	Ms. Nym Bjorkland, *New York, New York*
MUFFY AND CHIP	Mrs. George Jenson, *Greenwich, Connecticut*
NATASHIA AND SPIKE	Cindy DiGiovanni, *Leonia, New Jersey*
NIKKO AND DAIQUIRI	B.A. "Sam" Sammons, *Atlanta, Georgia*
99 AND SATCH	Mollie Stieglitz, *North Woodmere, New York*
OMAR AND NEWTON	Anne and Art Stiles, *New York, New York*
ORIS AND REFLECTION	The Goldman Family, *New York, New York*
PETE AND CATTY	Abigail and Arthur Morrison, *Riverdale, New York* (in the office of Howard Kessler DVM, New York, New York)
PIXIE AND RHETT	Frankie and Betty Price, *Lawrenceville, Georgia*
POO-POO AND BONES	Cindy Kate, *Atlantic City, New Jersey*
POPCORN AND HAMBURGER	Caroline and Don Harkleroad, *Atlanta, Georgia*
PRIDE AND JOY	Barbara E. Schmidt, *Leonia, New Jersey*
PSYCHE AND ATHENA	Debra, Rochelle and Bill Yates, *New York, New York*
PUTSCHKE AND PETE	Joan and Howard Baron, *New York, New York*
RAMSES II AND DANIEL	Gloria Jones, *Sagaponack, New York*
RASTUS AND ROCK	Gloria Hanks, *Tucker, Georgia*
RERE AND LILI	Liselotte and Simon Weyl, *New York, New York*

RHETT AND **SAMMIE**	Frankie and Betty Price, *Lawrenceville, Georgia*
SAMMY SABLE AND **SHEBA**	Janet A. Kennedy, M.D., *New York, New York*
SANCHO PANZA AND **DULCINEA**	Kimberly Goff, *Bridgehampton, New York*
SIRIO AND **SCHLOMO**	Ann and Roone Arledge, *New York, New York*
SLY OF FOXTAIL AND **BOO**	Jean-Claude Mastriani, *New York, New York*
SMOKEY AND **SUNNY**	Gil and Alecia Brown, *Atlanta, Georgia*
SOX AND **FLUFFERNUT**	Joan Summit, *Water Mill, New York*
TAIPAN AND **LAMA**	Eleanor Friede, *Bridgehampton, New York*
TARRAH AND **PETE**	Karen Kluglein and James D. Baron, *Bridgehampton, New York*
TURBO AND **PITTYWITS**	Anonymity requested.
TUXEDO AND **RAPUNZEL**	Alice F. Cohen, *Atlanta, Georgia*
WAIF AND **STRAY**	Abigail and Arthur Morrison, *Riverdale, New York*
WOODY AND **SPOT**	Craig and Susan Winters, *Atlanta, Georgia*